This Book
Belongs To:

My dear coloring enthusiasts!

Brissa Ocean is an independent brand that offers a wide range of different drawings, each carefully crafted to allow you to express yourself in the best way

We sincerely hope you enjoy coloring these unique images
and achieve a moment of calm and relaxation from the stress of daily life

These are just a few examples of what you'll find in this coloring book

Thank you for purchasing this coloring book, if you enjoyed your journey coloring these images, please consider taking a few minutes of your time to leave your opinion.
This means a great deal to me and I hope other people will benefit from it as well.

Thank you for purchasing this coloring book, if you enjoyed your journey coloring these images, please consider taking a few minutes of your time <u>to leave your opinion.</u>
This means a great deal to me and I hope other people will benefit from it as well.

Made in United States
Troutdale, OR
02/10/2024